Frayed Edges

Margaret Clark

Frayed Edges

Acknowledgements

My thanks for encouragement go to the community of Friendly Street Poets, my creative writing companions and my church community (where poems have become songs). Much love goes to my large and boisterous family who have been the inspiration for many poems but also keep me grounded.

Special thanks go to Alison Flett for her mentorship and sharing her knowledge.

Some poems in this collection have been previously published in the following anthologies:
'People Watching in a City Café' and 'Voyage of the Lady L' – *It's All Write*, JYC Anthology 1
'Hunter Gatherer' – *Flying Kites, Friendly Street Poets 36*
'Mixed Media' – *Patterns of Living, Friendly Street Poets 37*
'Second Drawer Down' – *The Infinite Dirt, Friendly Street Poets 38*
'Slowly Winding Down' – *Silver Singing Streams, Friendly Street Poets 39*
'The iCloud' – *Many Eyes, Many Voices, Friendly Street Poets 40*

Frayed Edges
ISBN 978 1 76041 229 6
Copyright © text Margaret Clark 2016
Cover image: Zoe Kennon
Photos: Nigel Clark

First published 2016 by
GINNINDERRA PRESS
PO Box 3461 Port Adelaide 5015
www.ginninderrapress.com.au

Contents

Of Earth and Water	9
Early Morning at Casuarina Beach	11
Shoreline	12
Cyclone	13
Autumn	16
Neptune	17
October Storm	18
Canticle in the Desert	20
The Voyage of the *Lady L*	21
Chaos Theory	24
Frayed Edges	27
Flat People	29
The Pool of Reflection	30
I Would if I Could	32
Bones	33
The Day the World Might End	34
Living on the Edge	36
Home Lands	37
Scotland and England – I	39
Scotland and England – II	41
Namatjira's Way	42
Feral Animal	44
Hunter Gatherer	46
Wattie Creek	47
Skin Deep	48
Belonging	49
Desert Dwelling	50
Return to Ireland	51

Hopes and Heresies — 53
- alone too long — 55
- Lines and Curves — 56
- Man, What is This Anger? — 57
- Church Music — 58
- The Holy Spirit, it is She — 59
- The Architect — 60
- Grace — 61
- Simon the Pharisee — 62
- The Chapel — 64
- Tenebrae — 65
- Washed in the Blood — 66

Meeting the Muse — 69
- Temptation — 71
- Mixed Media — 72
- Artists' Folly,   Haibun — 73
- One Night Stands — 76
- Night Visitor — 77
- Looking For Inspiration — 78
- Poetry and Pictures — 80
- On Viewing the Art of Anna Platten — 81
- The Birth of Magic — 82
- Waiting at the Station — 84

Just This Side of Indigo — 85
- Migraine — 87
- Old Friends — 88
- Colouring Books — 90
- Explain To Me Pain — 91
- Labyrinth — 92
- Fulfilling My Ambition — 93
- Dust on the Photograph — 96

Slowly Winding Down	97
Crosswords	98

Domestic Pleasures — 101

Doing Dishes	103
Second Drawer Down	104
Suburbia	105
Grandchild	106
Family Visit	107
School Days	108
Things that Make for a Happy Life	110
House Husband	112
Early Saturday Morning	114
You Are Young	116
Home Alone	118

Love and Other Catastrophes — 119

Dining Out	121
Falling	122
Directions	124
Love's Undertow	126
Imposter	128

Defying Gravity — 129

Exercise	131
People-watching in a City Café	132
Growing Up	134
The iCloud	136
A Certain Age	138

Of Earth and Water

Early Morning at Casuarina Beach

Darwin 1999

A fire hawk
scribes a lazy helix
in the morning air.

Pale gold sand is patterned
like Florentine tapestry,
intricately beaded
by a guild of master crabs.

Sky, so blue it hurts the eyes,
fades to off-white
as it meets the turquoise sea.

Grey-green casuarinas
fuss and whisper
in the breeze.

Children splash colour
on the pastel scene.
Squeal, as land and water
squabble over boundaries
around their feet.

And a wet sandy baby,
swaddled in her father's arms
shivers in excitement.

Such promise
in this fresh new day.

Shoreline

Denarau Island, Viti Levu, Fiji

A series of grand hotels are strung
like pearls along the shoreline.
Boulder walls and manicured lawns
where mangroves used to be.

The beach below is narrow,
and at the spring tide
the ocean rushes to the rocks,
swirls, foams and scours away the sand.

The roots of grass and palms
are exposed to the elements.
Trees that lost their battle with the ocean
litter the beach like dead soldiers.

The locals say it didn't used to be like this.
The beach was wider, still visible at high tide.
They shake their heads, talk about climate change
and the rising of the sea.

Further along the beach, beyond the resorts,
mangroves and palms still happily survive.
The beach is wide and clean
and free of driftwood.

Shore management is not
rocket science.
It is much more complicated.

Cyclone

Darwin 1998

Thelma threatens and frightens
and exhilarates the air.
Horizontal rain drives Darwin
to its knees, again.

My daughter is there, bravado in her voice,
the baby fretting in the background.
Twenty-four years ago she was a baby herself,
less than a year old, battered by Tracy.

Adrenalin is rushing through my veins
and I am frightened for her, reliving the horror.

The wind, the shattered glass,
the noise of sheet metal tearing from the roof.
Wet plasterboard collapsing round our heads.

Walls swaying, windows shattering
as I held the restless baby in my arms.
The dark, broken only by the spears of neon lightning.

The morning scape of devastation.
The four-by-two hurled through the cot
where the baby had slept only hours before.

Curtains caught beneath fallen walls
flapping like flags of surrender
in the diminishing wind.
Broken homes, naked trees and naked lives.

Blankets spread over bodies on the floorboards.
Power poles bent like hot melted candles.
A city littered with tinsel and wrapping paper.

The high of surviving, the camaraderie of shared loss
giving way to grief and anger.
Bravery and fear mixed like oil and water,
volatile and dangerous.

A city of dirty desperate people.
The looting of the shops.
Trolleys piled high with unnecessities.

The dogs turned feral, hungry and dangerous,
shot in front of children
and dumped in trenches with our effluent.

After three days, escape.
The Hercules flight,
seven hours of unremitting noise.
Speech impossible.
Seven hours to stare
at blood and bruises,
smell the stench of dysentery
and untreated wounds.

The spectacle of homeless souls
rushed from plane to transport
waiting on the tarmac,
avoiding the airport full of media
anxious to feed on our despair.

The ambulance sirens
through the city streets.
The bottles, drips and hushed voices
in the hospital ward.

Wet eyes and dry breasts,
nothing to feed my child.
Father left behind.

She doesn't know,
she doesn't remember,
unconscious then,
unknowing now.

History repeating.
Please God, no.
Don't do this to them.

Autumn

Spring and summer
are bleached away,
worn into slow
dull autumn.

The sun, pale and indifferent.
Pewter clouds
scud across cold skies,

flickering, sepia
movies of memories
bringing no passion.

I feel as
dry and brittle
devoid of living green
as autumn leaves.

Gather me, pile me high
and let me feel
the warmth of summer
in the heat of fire.

Neptune

At the breakwater, Candi Dasa, Bali

Tremble as Neptune roars.
He hisses and spits,
explodes in raging foam
above the breakwater.

Allied with time and tide
he will destroy
this artefact of lesser beasts
who trespass his domain.

He clears the jump
and races for the shore,
a thoroughbred in hues of blue
and phosphorescent white.

And almost spent,
returns to deep,
still fighting and clawing
and rattling the coral bones.

October Storm

Alice Springs

Mid-afternoon,
the air is charged.
Fresh sky of morning
aged to grey.

The hills
have lost their sharpness,
colours dulled,
like faded photographs.

Street lights, in response,
emit a feeble orange glow.
Haloes in the dusty air.

Wind is pulling at rusty nails
and rattling the fences.

Wattles shed their powdered gold
and jacarandas lilac tears.

Rain, in slow fat drops
steams from the hot earth,
releasing the desert's perfume.

Now heavier, driven by wind,
it pounds and roars on tin.
Soaks the thirsty earth
and cools the air.

Quiet and calm now.
Over all too soon.
Trees, heavy laden, droop their heads.
Water drips from corrugations.

Time suspended, reawakes.
White moths condense in clouds
around the she-oaks.
Birds return
and blue
breaks through the grey.

Canticle in the Desert

Dust storms over Alice Springs

When the sky is red
with dust over the desert,
there are voices in the wind
and in the storm.

Give me ears to hear,
and a heart to understand.

It is my life which is arid,
parched of meaning,
drained of purpose
and left to drift like dunes.

Give me ears to hear,
and a heart to understand.

I seek out pleasures
in possessions and distractions,
yet joy eludes me
and I want someone to blame

Give me ears to hear,
and a heart to understand.

Teach me to seek the joy in every day
and peace will follow.
Help me to see the goodness
in my neighbours and myself.

Take my arid life
and teach me to love.
Settle the dust
and let the desert bloom.

The Voyage of the *Lady L*

Inspired by *Poem 4* of Catullus
and the Islands of the Whitsunday Passage

In Airlie Beach the boats, all glist'ning white
await our keen arrival at the quay,
and *Lady L*, most elegant of cats,
will be our craft, our haven on the sea.

Provisions stowed and briefing underway,
we study charts and make ourselves at home.
Then safely round the rock walls, out to sea,
the pilot's gone and we are now alone.

We've waited long to find this time of year
when Jove is kindly to a novice crew.
No timber now, but fibreglass and steel
to face the ocean's hundred moods of blue.

We distance from the shore and set a course
with engines stilled and mainsail strained alee.
Then, moored and rested, toast the setting sun.
Stonehaven for the night, our first at sea.

Day one of our adventure so soon gone.
Our crew of four, we share a fine repast,
play cards, and read and talk the evening through;
a night beneath the stars, on darkness cast.

The sun, she rises misty with the dawn.
It warms and clears, reveals the brand new day.
Thank God for rest, for guidance as we sail
between the shoals and into Blue Pearl Bay.

All dressed in black, we masquerade as seals,
explore the alien world that ripples mask.
With silent gestures, share the wonders there.
Soft corals sway, as fish and turtles pass.

The Bay of Butterflies has earned its fame
for stunning coral bommies close to shore.
Below the water once again we slip,
besotted with the beauty, seeking more.

The day is ageing fast, before our eyes,
we sail once more, to beat the evening light.
We're heading north past Cateran and steer
to Saba Bay, to anchor for the night

At rest, our *Lady* dances with the swell.
The anchor chain is struggling and complains.
The light upon the masthead swings on stars.
Our cradle rocks and carries us on dreams.

Whitehaven Beach, the priceless jew'l next day
appears in palest gold and sapphire blue.
Our photographs, her spirit compromise?
But no, her shifting sands sculpt each day new.

Next day we wake to raindrops on the hatch
and leave our sheltered bay for heavy seas.
The jib is furled, the hulls are lost in spray
as dark waves rise to swamp the trampoline.

Hatches! Sheets! Trav'ller! Cleats! they yell.
The tell tales horizontal in the gale.
The men and *Lady L* are overjoyed
to have this opportunity to sail!

Apollo, she of Sydney–Hobart fame,
sails past us, kevlar straining in the wind.
Through Solway Passage, where the current's strong,
until a shelter for the night we find.

Chance Bay, so peaceful after such a ride.
We celebrate with olives, wine and cheese.
We raise a glass to Flinders and to Cook,
give thanks for *Lady L*, for wind and seas.

The days go by, we talk, we swim, we sail
around the horn of Pentecost, past Molle.
Two whales, a mother and her calf, we sight
just south of Lindeman. We've done it all!

We've sailed our hundred magic miles; now home,
returning *Lady L* to Airlie's shore.
But we'll be back, by Jove. We'll dream and plan,
for this cat's crew are novices no more.

Chaos Theory

A while back now,
a blue butterfly
was seen flying
into a corn field
in Alabama.

Over the following few years
there was a significant rise
in sea temperature
off the east coast of Australia,
coral bleaching
on the Great Barrier Reef
and a southerly migration
of tropical fish.

There was another sighting
of the butterfly
(although some witnesses
said it was a dragonfly)
over a duck pond in Sussex.

Less than a week later
great chunks of pale green ice
fell into the ocean
off the arctic coast.

And just the other day
the blue butterfly was seen
near an irrigation channel
in China.

Within twenty-four hours
there were three wild fires
burning out of control
in the hills to the east of LA.

Which just goes to show
the interconnectedness
of everything.

It is a most attractive theory.
We can blame the chaos butterfly
and do nothing.

Frayed Edges

Flat People

Look at them
up there
on the catwalk.

Showing their ribs
and shoulder blades
and gaps between their legs.

Flat women,
two-dimensional people,
paper dolls in cut-out clothes.

Turn them sideways,
and they cast no shadow,
close the glossy magazine
and they disappear.

I'd rather be a woman
curved and comfortable,
happy in my flesh
and not afraid to eat.

The Pool of Reflection

Hyde Park War Memorial, Sydney

In the park there stands
a towering monument to valour.
Domes and columns carved in marble,
statues cast in bronze,

steps that rise for men who fall,
and as a counter to the strength
of stone and metal,
there lies a liquid mirror to this vanity.

A stately guard of poplars
flanks the pool,
salutes inverted images of war
remembered, glorified.

The wooden soldiers cry.
Single leaves, as green and keen
as new recruits, dive and die
in the reflected glory.

Captains of industry
no time for contemplation
march to their destination
across the park.

Heels click, clack, staccato, stark
against the traffic's symphonies

And on a park bench in the shade
a solitary soldier spends his day
and I can't help asking
Is there any glory in surviving?

I Would if I Could

I would if I could
turn back the clock and make my body
look like it did before I had babies, only six inches taller.

I would if I could,
if only they would stand me on a podium
and crown me Miss Universe; I have my speech ready.

I would if I could
give everyone in the world clean drinking water,
nutritious food, good health and their three score years and ten.

I would if I could
give them all a loving family, a safe home
and a happy community.

I would if I could
give all kids as much education as they could absorb
and the chance throughout life to keep learning.

I would if I could
melt down all the weapons in the world
and swap them for dignity and kindness.

I would if I could
find fulfilling work for all who are able
and a reasonable day's pay for their efforts.

I would if I could
make all these things happen
as long as it didn't mean lowering my standard of living.

Bones

Every time I write,
I reveal
a few more bones:

A lower mandible
which moves too much,
says things it shouldn't say.

Phalanges which point
in accusation
or clench in idle threats.

A humerus waiting for a joke,
an ulna to dig you in the ribs,
ribs that rise and fall in impatient sighs.

Femurs trying to hang out with the hip crowd
but end up getting involved with dodgy patellas
or just making a dash for it when things get tough.

Tarsals and metatarsals
poised ready to kick
at all the idiocy of life,

revealing my own prejudices
and fears,
the skeletons in my closet.

The Day the World Might End

21 December 2012, the last day on the Mayan calendar

Day dawns blue and clear.
Temperatures predicted for the mid-twenties.
A perfect day and I promise myself
not to waste it.

Plans are already thwarted in a nice way
with a cup of tea in bed.
But we have visitors,
good manners say I'd better get up.

My husband's mother and brother
are here to celebrate Mum's 86th birthday
and Christmas
on the off-chance the world lasts that long.

Breakfast is nothing special.
Tea or coffee, cereal or toast.
Nobody wants eggs or pancakes.
No real sense of occasion.

Ordinary domestic chores,
dishes, laundry.
Further cups of tea, accompanied by mince pies
just in case we can't enjoy them later.

My daughter-in-law arrives with her littlies.
Mum is delighted.
She hasn't met the baby before,
her eighth great-grandchild.

Lunch is uneventful. I cook mushroom pies,
which the adults enjoy but the children won't eat.
Nothing new there.
No signs yet of impending doom, whatever that looks like.

The afternoon is quiet. The kids have gone home.
The brothers are chatting; they don't see each other often.
Mum is resting. I clear up toys and dishes, mop the kitchen floor.
The sky is still a brilliant blue, a few soft clouds on the horizon.

This evening we head for the hills, to Lobethal's lights,
to add a little sparkle and bling to this momentous day.
Visit the markets where my daughter and granddaughter
are selling their art to those who believe in tomorrow.

A cold evening after a warm day.
Junk food from roadside stalls.
A nativity play with gentle alpacas
instead of bad-tempered camels. Nice touch.

We tour the Christmas lights, winding our way through the hills,
past the Chain of Ponds where the water level is getting low.
Mum is very tired and heads straight to bed when we get home.
'You wait till you're nearly 86,' she says.

I think she'll make it to her birthday. Tomorrow will surely come.
Another day to balance precariously
on the 31,408 she has already had.
But I don't know. It's not midnight yet.

Living on the Edge

Sitting alone beside the Brisbane River,
after moving from Central Australia

I am at the edge
building a new life.

Behind me the desert
and the ancient hills

that hold my history
and a portion of my soul.

Ahead, the river and the shore
and friends I haven't met yet.

The net
that held me in safety
and comfort for so long
is gone.

Old friends are words on paper
voices on the phone.

How I miss them,
my independence
and my comfort zone.

I live on edge
watching for tomorrow

building a new life
and waiting,

waiting for my muse
to wake and follow.

Home Lands

Scotland and England – I

On the eve of the referendum for Scottish independence,
September 2014

She has always been a feisty woman.
and he a bit of a bully.
I thought, though,
they had sorted things out.

At least the physical violence is over,
but there is more to it than that,
more forms of abuse
than sword or arrow.

Too tight on the purse strings,
perhaps, too many put downs.
Him always looking over her shoulder.
to see if she's getting things right.

Is he still a jealous lover,
a misogynist,
wary of her ability
to stand up for herself?

Maybe she doesn't need
a breadwinner any more.
We, her children, are grown,
independent.

I don't want them to split.
I love them both,
my mother land and father land
despite their faults.

But I understand
where she is coming from.
There is too much history
to simply forget.

Scotland and England – II

On the eve of the referendum for Scottish independence,
September 2014

Passions are high
in the Palace of Westminster
and the Halls of Holyrood.

Opinions lay on lips
in London cabs
and in the warp and weft
of Edinburgh streets.

Nelson watches, silent,
from his lofty perch
and Wallace from his tower
above the Bridge of Allan.

But these are the lands
of Shakespeare, Scott and Burns.
This time it is a battle
not of swords but words.

We can take heart, be comforted
so gently, by these nations
who build their greatest monuments
not to warriors but to bards.

Namatjira's Way

From Alice Springs to Hermannsburg after heavy winter rain

The rainbow serpent* sleeps
along the golden mile.

Great bony plates arise
from a body scaled in shades
of amethyst and jade.

Shivering and shimmering
in the chilly wind,
the creature stirs.

Silver sennas,
by autumn rains
are Midas-touched to gold.

Spinifex grows in spikes
of emerald among
the serpent's fallen scales.

Budgerigars fly
in formation
between ghost gum and she-oak,

moving in air
like neons in water,
fragments of opal on the wing.

A filigree of pewter cloud
wanders the sapphire sky,
softens the desert light.

Such a land of jewels,
rough cut and beautiful,
gives birth to art and dreaming.

* The MacDonnell Ranges west of Alice Springs are known by the traditional owners, the Arrernte people, as the Rainbow Serpent.

Feral Animal

Fur the colour of dappled shadows
adapted to the she-oaks and the spinifex.
Surviving on birds and lizards.
Cunning and scrawny on the meagre fare.

Yellow eyes,
infected with hard life,
the colour of urine
in a land too dry.

The hunter becomes the prey.

The white man,
who brought you
to this black man's land,
admonishes your cruelty
to the native fauna.

He lifts his rifle
to his sight,
savouring the conquest
and the kill.

The trigger squeezed,
the dappled body jumps,
shocked into death.

Muscles twitch
and come to rest.

The feral man,
to hide his pleasure,
justify his blood lust,

says, ignorant of irony,
you have no right
to be here.

Hunter Gatherer

We took your land
and gave you tea and sugar.
We took your hunting
and gave you bags of flour.

We brought our God
and laughed at the Guditja.
Scoffed at pitjuri
and gave you wine.

Your feet that trod the land
have no where else to go.

You hunt and gather now
the only way you can.
Your hand, that held the spear,
outstretched and waiting.

Wattie Creek

The return of native lands, 1975, Wave Hill, NT

Sands drift down
to measure time
and measure what is lost.

Dust returned
from hand to hand,
from white to black,
from Whitlam
back to Lingiari.

This dust defiled.
This dust devoid
of dreaming.

Skin Deep

I cannot know you for
I live within this skin.

And though I do not always
wear it well,
I can wear no other.

You live in yours
and I in mine

This may be our first
and only sin.

Belonging

Indigenous, what does that mean?
You're black, I'm white.
All our kids were born here
in the red centre.

We've both seen the river change
from dry sand
to raging torrent,

lived through the dust storms
and tasted the grit,

have the red dirt
ingrained in our feet.

And the hills
that wrap around us,
like the Rainbow Serpent,

they are part
of my dreaming too.
I'm a part of them.

Where else shall I go?

Desert Dwelling

'the ocean
reminds me of my death
and the fact that it need not be fatal'
– Erica Jong, from *I live in New York*

I love the ocean,
tranquil or passionate,
summer green or winter grey.

She is my soulmate,
my unrequited love.
The ebb and flow reflection
of my life and death
and resurrection.

So why do I live
a thousand miles
from tides?

Perhaps the wanting
and the waiting
stir my soul
and bring the words.

Happiness would be too easy
and peace is like a drug.
It puts my muse to sleep.

Return to Ireland

June 2013

I came to Ireland as a tiny child
wild eyed and foreign,
to words I hardly understood
and yet was welcomed.

Five years had past,
a happy childhood spent
when restless parents
again were up and went.

And I, as green
as Ireland itself,
set sail for southern lands
with no regret.

In later years, I've felt
this quiet yearning,
yet half a century passed
till my returning.

And here once more
I know what I have missed,
the green, the cool,
the mountains, lakes and mist.

I love the humour of the Irish soul,
the pipes, the fiddle and the Irish air.
It's filled an empty place in me
I didn't even realise was there.

Hopes and Heresies

alone too long

meditation on creation

alone
you form the world
and sigh

light and dark
mountains
lakes and skies

stars travel
in their ordained path
and time begins
unseen

it works well
the ground swells
green

a company of creatures
rise
upon your word

on land and sea and sky
as yet unheard

and in your image
us, the last
approved and blessed

are you less lonely
in your rest?

Lines and Curves

'I was frightfully fond of the universe and wanted to address it by a diminutive. I often did so; and it never seemed to mind.'
– G.K. Chesterton, *Orthodoxy*

Euclid, Pythagoras, Newton
sensed the music of the universe,
poetry in nature, art in numbers.

Enamoured by a sine curve,
a graceful hyperbola or parabola,
besotted by asymptotes and axes,
cones, like wizards' hats,
carved and sliced.

The magic revealed
but diminished
in quadratic equations.

Lines and curves, always seeking,
never finding one another.
Distances so large, so small.
No infinity, no zero.

Always closer to the truth
but never there,
even at the speed of light.

Man, What is This Anger?

A response to the Serbian–Albanian conflict in Kosovo, 1999

Man, what is this anger
that you vent upon your brother?
Who is this God you're calling?
Yahweh, Allah, Abba, I am one.

Abraham, I blessed him
and both his sons, I spared them
(Isaac from the alter, Ishmael from lack of water)
and I cried and died beside you all
when you took my gentle son.

Jews and Gentiles, Christians, Pagans,
Muslims, Infidels and Heathens,
it is all misunderstanding,
holy wars, you blame on me.

Surrender hate and weapons
for in war there are no winners.
Spare your mothers and your sisters
and set your children free.

Church Music

In honour of George Herbert

Where else can I go
to lift my voice in song
and not be silenced?
Only God will take
my joyful noise
without critique.

To worship God
is more a pleasure than a duty
when music takes me
from the daily tasks
and lifts my heart to his mystique.

In this there is no bar
to separate the rich and poor,
joined together in a song of praise.

Sunday, just a little touch of heaven
to feed the heart and soul,
to live in love on all the other days.

The Holy Spirit, it is She

On reading the prayers of Julian of Norwich

The Holy Spirit
It is she
who lifts me up
from my despair
to glimpse beyond
the troubles of today
and whispers softly in my ear
'This too will pass
and all is well.'

The Architect

My working world is full
of straight lines
and geometric curves
carefully drawn and
carefully measured.

Your world is drawn freehand.
No two trees or leaves
or creatures alike.

And yet there is a pattern
in your awesome creation,
a sureness and security.

A sense both of uniqueness
and belonging to the whole.

Grace

Inspired by the writing of Phillip Yancey

I am the lost coin,
the lost sheep,
the wayward child,
found and forgiven.

Hear the laughter
and pleasure at my return.

I come to the banquet
in my travelling clothes.
Drink living water turned to wine
and eat all manna of good things.

I work an hour in the afternoon
and am paid for the day.

Unfair you say, unfair!
Why settle for fair,
when I am offered grace?

Simon the Pharisee

Luke 7:36-50

I have asked him to my home, this preacher man,
to understand his message and his powers.
To take him from the pressing crowds
for just a few short hours.

I yearn to delve beyond the tales
and wild speculation,
to seek His God, of so much more
than rules and regulations.

But instead of quiet time together, listening,
a crowd has gathered in my home,
and now this woman, black hair glistening,
kneels at his feet, praying, weeping.

For all his wisdom, he doesn't seem to know
a woman such as this can bring him down
and all her fine perfume cannot cleanse
or her past deeds drown.

He looks at me and sees my soul,
speaks my name and reads my thoughts
and, to my shame, compares her sins to mine
and I have no recourse.

He talks of hospitality and praises her
tears and perfume mingled with a hint of myrrh.
Her heart is filled with love
and mine so poor.

Remorse and yearning tame
my turmoil and my anger.
To know this Jesus is to face
my poverty and hunger.

The Chapel

Early morning at Woolaston Chapel, Perth

I went to your house this morning
and thought you weren't at home.
I tried and couldn't see you
in the coloured glass and stone.
But the tears dried and the pain eased
and I wasn't so alone.

Tenebrae

Service of the Shadows, Maundy Thursday

I am held in vigil
by the candle light,
haloed round
by my unfocused sight.

Seven flames, then five,
then three and one
and then the darkness
of the deeds I've done.

Your heart is breaking
in the midnight frost.
Your son, my light
is almost lost.

While I yearn
the golden warmth of noon,
your grace shines silver
in the haloed moon.

Washed in the Blood

A word to Jesus about a priest who couldn't cope with 'women's business'

The dull heaviness grows
and slows me down.
The ache becomes a pain
as if my belly has melted
to my thighs
and then been ripped asunder.

With the phases of the moon
this pain has waxed and waned
for nigh on thirty years.

And all my sisters share
my cycle and my plight,
each in her own measure.

*

Your blood was shed for me
and for many,
forgiving sins.

Ours is shed for you
and for all,
for giving birth.

Your blood is sanctified
and there is glory
in your pain.

Mine is unclean
must stay unseen
and my pain borne
in secrecy and shame.

>   *

Yet the man stands there
in his pristine white,
a priest to represent you
in your sacrifice.
Unknowing of the pain,
unstained,
yet only gods and women
bleed and live again.

Meeting the Muse

Temptation

When I read too much
there is always a temptation
to steal.

Sneak out in the dead of night
dressed in black skivvy,
jeans and a balaclava,
equipped with a torch
and a pair of sharp scissors.

Coming home before dawn
with other poets' gems
in a pillowcase.

Even this idea,
I stole from Billie Collins.

How proud would I be
if someone stole
a word or phrase from me,
on the assumption that imitation
is the sincerest form of flattery.

That only the talented
get plagiarised.
So please, Mr Collins,
don't be cross.

Mixed Media

A poem for Alison

I used to write in watercolour,
masking highlights, reserving white,
starting in the pale and moving to the dark.
Wet on wet to paint a euphemism,
soften the meaning,
Wet on dry, the hard-edged truth.
Fast drying words,
transparent, unchangeable.
Always following the rules,
the unbending rules.

But I am learning instead
to write my poetry in oils.
Mixing, tinting, blending, hinting
at happiness in cadmium, passion in vermilion,
sorrow in ochre, serenity in phthalo blue.
I am intoxicated with the smell of words,
listening for shades of Payne's grey.
Tasting the metre, moulding the phrases,
soft and malleable, on my tongue.
Taking time to work them, change them,
or sit back relaxed and uncommitted,
giving them space to settle.

And while I give my pen a brief sabbatical,
I'll mix myself a metaphor,
and drink a toast to colour and to words.

Artists' Folly, Haibun

Montsalvat Artists' Colony, Eltham, Victoria

Entering the gallery, my eyes adjust to the gloomy light. In the entry hall, artists past and present gaze into the room where old and new mingle, sharing the walls. Old Dutch-style masters occupy much of the space and the mood, detailed, exquisite, but oh so dark.

As for the rest of the exhibition, they are contemporary and abstract. I peer and squint, close up and far away, and turn my head at every angle, but I fail to engage except for maybe one or two. Rather uninspired, I re-emerge into the gardens on the other side.

> And then the magic happens.
> The world is folded
> to an origami butterfly
> and centuries are Dali'd
> to fit beneath its wings.

Crumbling stucco, rusting roofs and broken windows are softened by the gold of autumn vines. The wattle and daub of Australian pioneers sit comfortably beside the brick infill timber frame of Shakespeare's England.

And then the stone, the beautiful stone, rough and rustic limestone, warm as a Tuscan summer. Or dark and formal granite, carved and arched over leadlight windows, as cold and threatening as a Norman invasion.

I enter the tiny chapel as clouds block out the winter sun, chilling to the bone, enquiring of the soul, but it is much too nice a day for Inquisitions. As I leave behind the heaviness of the chapel, the sun finds an opening in the curtain of cloud.

> Back to the Heidelberg light
> of this gentle day,
> where geese in an adjacent field
> relive McCubbin's *Winter Evening*.

The gardens are graced with sculptures, abstract and modern, classical and whimsical, a hint of Norman Lindsay in the almond eyes.

Shady stone arches give glimpses of sunlit gardens. Stone steps lead to a tower where an artist chats with the blacksmith from the forge below.

> And in the sculptor's studio,
> among the chips of rock,
> half finished works
> await the chisel and the vision.

Through dusty windows we see silk flowers and wax fruit, artfully arranged for a still life masterpiece.

Another arch invites, and I step through to a courtyard with a swimming pool, slightly green, with ancient plumbing, and on the terrace above, wrought-iron tables and chairs, shaded by vines.

> It only needs the patrons,
> strong coffee and sweet pastries,
> snippets of conversation *en Française*.
> All my notions of Provence rolled into one.

On to the main hall for medieval banqueting. A solitary artist with her oils, captures on canvas the warm rich English oak and Welsh slate, bathed in the dusty shafts of light filtered through stippled glass.

My imagination peoples the hall with merry knights and fills the tables with bread and fruit and great slabs of beef.

> Tall tales of quixotic deeds
> and Holy Grails,
> embellished and cheered
> over tankards of beer
> around the crackle and glow
> of a blazing fire.

What a magical place. Grand tours to Europe may be just a dream, but I can write and paint and reminisce, for I have been to Montsalvat.

One Night Stands

'Oh for an art that is not made of words
with all their odours and indiscretions.'
– Erica Jong, *The Poetry Suit*

Shame on the poet
who writes nonsense
and calls it art.

Treating words like whores
and blackening
their good name.

Let the words
wear their own clothes,
bring their own baggage.

Romance them.
Dance with them lightly.
Just don't strip them
of dignity
and meaningful relationships.

Night Visitor

The muse arrives at two a.m.
on nights I am most weary.
Bids me seek a pen and pad
and as I write I hear she
offers gems of puns and plays
to make the poets jealous.

But only in the small dark hours
will she deem to tell us
things of life and love
of wisdom, rhyme and metre,
things not privy to the day.
Fatigue is the creator.

And should I wait in warmth
till light of day has grown,
the muse is gone,
the words, the song
have faded with the dawn.

Looking For Inspiration

With help from Emily Dickinson and Peter Goldsworthy

Some dark days
I feel that
all the good poems
have already been written.

Themes of love and loss,
summer rain, spring blossoms;
what is there left to say?

Maybe something edgy
about freedom fighters
and radicals?

A little sexism and racism
to shock?

Something hilariously funny
about politics?

Poignant stories of childhood?
Its all been done.

Done to…
bored to…
death.

That's another theme.
Nothing new there.

Death, grief, loss.
Don't want to go that way.

Why can't I write like…

Who are my chosen few?
Emily who says, 'Hope is a thing with feathers.'
Peter who asks, 'Must all things be explained?'
says, 'There is nothing as empty as the future.'

Empty in a good way,
a blank canvas, a clean sheet,
a million possibilities.

Perhaps there is room
in the world
for a few more poems.

Poetry and Pictures

Why is my poetry
so often the product
of a troubled mind?

My patron,
the muse of melancholy.

Normal, happy days
are not expressed
too readily in words.

A moment to enjoy
with superficial thought
and not be laboured or recorded.

But misery will wallow,
analyse itself,
seek its source, pick the scabs
and save it all in lengthy verse.

Poetry tips the scales,
unbalances the true picture.

Thank goodness for the camera
and the happy candid photographs
to set the record straight.

On Viewing the Art of Anna Platten

Exhibition *The Devil is in the Detail* at the SA Art Gallery, October 2012

They are huge these canvasses
and that shouldn't be important
but it is right now
as I struggle myself with big pictures.

The physical difficulty
of getting to the heart of things.

And the art, the talent,
the detail
where you say the devil hides.

Not true.
There are far more angels than devils
in your work.

Skin, so soft and warm
I sense a pulse in that slender wrist,
a heartbeat beneath the Edwardian gown.

Fur, velvet, lace; all so real
I want to feel the texture,
run my hand over the timber toys,
draw my finger along a spider's web.

I am besotted by your stories
and your gifts, Anna Platten,

entranced by your talent,
drawn into your three-dimensional world
on a two-dimensional plane.

The Birth of Magic

'Woman is not a poet, she is either a muse or she is nothing... She should be the visible moon; impartial, loving, severe, wise'
– Robert Graves, from *The White Goddess*

Born as a shaft of light
against the indigo,
the Virgin Goddess
travels by the stars.

Then maidenhead surrendered
to the glorious Sun,
she swells and glows
and draws

the life force
of the women
and the oceans
to her soul.

When night is alive,
awash in sterling silver,
the Goddess, gravid,
awaits the birth of Magic.

And as she sheds
the blood of life
and sacrifice,
she fades to red.

Back bent to nurse the child,
the Goddess ages,
turns her face away
and darkness overcomes the light.

But as the Magic grows,
the child
becomes a woman,
a poet and a muse.

And in the crescent
of her mother's fading youth
she rests and rocks
and waits for wisdom.

Waiting at the Station

Is there any way to know
how to make the luck happen,
be there when the opportunities
are handed out?

They say the more you practice
the luckier you get.
But how many great songs are written
that no one will ever sing?

How many great stories
are hidden in bottom drawers
or get shredded with all the other paperwork
when the relatives clear out the attic?

How many paintings of great beauty
hide in cupboards
while *Blue Poles* hangs
in the National Gallery?

I'll be waiting at the railway station
when my boat comes in.

Just This Side of Indigo

Migraine

Be still, be dark, be quiet.
All else is pain

that washes
in waves of grey
across the cranium.

Tinnitus drones a forest
of cicadas in my ears.
Naught else I hear.

To move is to tilt
the world to vertigo,
the pain to indigo.

To see is to change
the pain
to blinding white.

I crave the night.
I beg for sleep,
for sweet oblivion.

Be still, be dark, be quiet.
All else is pain.

Old Friends

Old friends are the best,
the ones that knew you
when you were young and pretty
and full of dreams.

Careers, happily ever afters,
babies. We did it all.

We weren't too ambitious
back then.
Fame and fortune
were never on our radar.

Despite the grey hair, the wrinkles,
the dodgy knees and the multifocals,
we could still see those young girls
we used to be.

As we shared cups of tea and memories
we laughed about our ageing sons,
as bald now as they were back then.

Boasted about grandchildren
all smart and pretty
and as full of tomorrow
as we are of yesterday.

'But I don't want to live through them,' I said,
much as I love them. 'What about us?
Now should have been our freedom years
of café culture, art and philosophy.'

I thought you agreed
but instead you gave in
to this old age nonsense.
And now you've gone.

I made a foolish mistake
saying goodbye
to that still body,
that deadly pallor.

I don't need that vision
to cloud my yesterdays with you.

And, as you descend to the ashes,
a whole treasury of 'remember when'
and 'what next'
is going up in smoke.

Colouring Books

I was traumatised
as a child
by colouring books.

While others wailed
because they could not
stay within the edges

I am still struggling
to break across the lines.

Explain To Me Pain

Explain to me pain,
a purpose
for the suffering.

Are we guilty
or are we chosen?
Punishment for the body
or instruction for the soul?

Thunder when we seek music,
too deaf perhaps,
to hear a quiet song of caution?

Question marks catch like fishing hooks
in my gasping mouth.
Barbs to tear the fabric
of a fragile faith.

No answers, only questions
and the pain.

Labyrinth

It is a labyrinth,
life's journey,
wrong turns, false starts
and blank walls along the way.

I can't see my destination,
but I know, as I turn and return,
that the blank walls
protect me from the cliff's edge.

And in each false start
there is a lesson
and a growing.

Along the way
I meet those
further on their journey
who share their light.

They move from their path
to make my going easier
and some can teach me
when it is safe
to cross the lines.

Fulfilling My Ambition

For my bipolar mother who died far too young

My ambition was born
of your demise, Mother.
In grief
I could feel myself spiralling
down that same rabbit hole.

Soon after you were gone, I turned thirty,
watched my youngest child go to school.
I could sense your despair,
feel myself slipping.

I didn't want to depend
on my man or my children
for happiness, or a reason to exist.

I didn't want to die
of over-inflated dreams
and unfulfilled promises.

So I studied hard, won awards,
learnt to visualise other people's dreams
in bricks and mortar.

My first project was to
built a wall around my heart
so it couldn't be bruised or broken,
quite as easily as yours.

I could immerse myself
in lines and curves and Rotring ink,
revel in the art of architecture.

I took pleasure in inspecting
damp proof membranes
and reinforcing steel
before an early morning concrete pour,

standing there with my clipboard,
dressing up the little girl
in hard hat and safety boots,

and even managing to fool
the workmen and myself into believing
that I had some authority.

But always at the edge of every building site
was the rabbit hole, sides crumbling,
and me, with dirty fingernails,
clawing my way back to the surface.

It's over now, the brilliant career,
and in hindsight
there were far more highs than lows.

I have backfilled the rabbit hole
but there is the occasional subsidence
so I don't forget.
It is always there in my peripheral vision.

After all these years,
the wall I built
around my heart has crumbled.
I won't rebuild it.

I find you were right all along, Mother,
despite the dangers.
The love of those I care about
is all that matters.

Dust on the Photograph

There is dust on the sepia photograph.
My mother in her army uniform
circa 1944.
She looks confident, serene.

Before husband and five kids.
Before depression and
too much medication.

Before being dragged
halfway round the world
by my restless, nomadic father.

There is dust on the sepia photograph,
the dust of broken promises
and eroded dreams.

Slowly Winding Down

A rondeau

She's slowly winding down, and yet aware
of family who claim that they still care,
yet not enough to keep her by their side;
instead, this nursing home where they can hide
her lack of dignity, and their despair.

Their own mortality, reflected there,
parchment skin, clouded eyes and thinning hair,
the truth of life, that no one can abide.
She's slowly winding down.

They visit now, but never time to spare,
a duty, born of memories she can't share,
and time has formed a gulf, a great divide.
The young play on, the old are set aside.
Both she and they are painfully aware
she's slowly winding down.

Crosswords

8 across

Her man left an hour ago for his job in the city.
Now she watches as the kids head for school.
Waves goodbye, eyes glazed,
staring at the street through net curtains.

She empties the dregs, boils the kettle
and makes herself another pot of tea.
Picks up the daily paper
and searches for the crossword puzzle.

10 across

Cholesterol for breakfast, chicken involved, pig committed.
Does the dishes, clears up the kids' lunch mess.
Puts on a load of washing. Another cup of tea perhaps?

11 across

Something stronger to soften the edges of the empty squares.
Another achievement, one little task pegged out to dry.
Maybe a movie on the telly.

12 down

How to blur the hours, shorten the day?
A tablet perhaps, two even better.

2 down

When is a rest a black hole?

4 down

kids home and a thumping headache.
Noise she can't cope with,
filling the squares with wrong answers.

6 down
Husband home,
perhaps he can take her black dog for a walk.
Or maybe not. Do problems go away if they're ignored?

7 down
From sea and earth, in yesterdays news.
What's for dinner when no one wants to cook?

8 down
Kids in bed, husband hidden behind a newspaper.
TV droning.

9 down
A word for loneliness in a crowd.

2 across
More effective than 12 down:
the wrists, the silent cry for help.
So many squares left blank.

Domestic Pleasures

Doing Dishes

I like doing dishes
If you do the job
often enough
it can be done
in Zen.

Warm sudsy water.
Karate kid action
with the dishcloth.

Metallic clunk of cutlery.
Fragile chink of glass.

Lulled by repetition
to an alpha wave.

Coffee pot space,
percolating ideas.

Thinking space,
as good as meditation.

Second Drawer Down

In my kitchen is a drawer
full of things
that don't fit anywhere else.

Rugged individuals
who aren't going to smarten up
for anything or anybody.

Little measuring spoons
from teaspoon to half-a-cup
that refuse to acknowledge
the hierarchy of things.

Miniature torture devices,
meat mallet, cheese grater,
garlic press, apple corer.

Knives that don't fit in the knife block,
a pie slicer, should I ever bake a pie,
tin opener, potato peeler,
my favourite little red handled paring knife.

Don't misunderstand.
These are all useful things.
I just wish they would stay tidy.

Their unruly behaviour
and lack of decorum
do my head in
and play havoc with my OCD.

Suburbia

Greetings and goodbyes.
Lawnmowers
on sleepy afternoons.

Car doors slamming.
Urgent whispers and
stifled laughter.
Angry fathers.

Close enough
to catch
snatches
of other people's lives.

Hear
their children's tantrums.
Smell their dinner.

See their intimates
upon the line
but never know
their names.

Grandchild

Emily, our Emily
you are all of two days old
at 4.08 a.m.

With angels' kisses
fresh upon your cheeks
and lips of porphyry,

already, you're adored
and have the power
to break my heart.

And as your mother
holds you in her arms
in wonderment and awe

I pray that she will know,
through knowing you,
how much I love her.

Family Visit

You are gone now
and the toys are packed away.

No more ducks in the bath tub
or your mother's make-up
sprawled across the vanity.

And we won't ask why
there was a cookie cutter
in the wood basket
and a yellow truck in my bed.

Enough said.

The coffee table is free of sticky fingerprints
and the fridge
of your mother's after dinner mints.
I suppose that's good.

No bottles on the drainer
or Vegemite on the cupboard doors.
Clean floors
where the borrowed highchair stood.

The cat has come down
from the top shelf,
she's almost her old self.

The smudges on the windows
I might leave for a while;
they make me smile.

The house is quiet and tidy now
and very, very dull.

School Days

Minding the grandkids while Mum and Dad have a holiday

An octopus of legs and arms invade my sleep.
Two tousled heads of blonde play tents beneath the sheet.
The sleeping tiger wakes and roars
and rattles at his bars to be released.

The tiger, freed, stampedes along the corridor
and stops abruptly at the pantry door.
He smiles and says 'dink pease' in such a way
it adds a little sunshine to the early morning grey.

So orange juice all round
and Weet-bix eaten
straight-legged on the ground
begin their day.

And then the dreaded early-morning tasks,
brushing teeth and hair and filling flasks.
Finding things for lunch that Em will eat,
into uniform and shoes on feet.

'I can't make my bed. It isn't fair!
Where's my book? I know I left it here!'
Tears and accusations are abated
when eventually her reader is located.

Emily, aged five, who's known it all
since she was three, looks up at me
and wondering if a tummy ache will do the trick
says 'Gran, I don't have to go to school if I am sick.'

This piece of insight I ignore.
We make it to the door
and down the stairs, a task that can't be hurried,
as Mr Nearly Two is much too independent
to be carried.

At school, when friends are found
all tears and sorrow
can be forgotten,
until this time tomorrow.

Things that Make for a Happy Life

Inspired by *The Means to Attain a Happy Life*,
Henry Howard, Earl of Surrey, 1516–47

A peaceful land in which to live,
where politicians know their place.
A comfortable home that's paid for soon,
a haven, from the constant race.

A husband, a friend, a lover combined,
a family to love and cheer you on.
Invading like they own the place,
who visit often, then go home.

Good work to do and time to do it,
to stretch the intellect and skills.
Satisfaction at a task complete,
recognition of a job done well.

The bills all paid, some cash left over,
enough, but steering clear of greed.
A little to spend on something pretty.
The means to help a friend in need.

A warm bed on a chilly night.
The right clothes for the right season.
A patch of sunshine on a winter's day.
A box of chocolates for no good reason.

A bounty from the vegie patch.
Good food to share, the occasional treat.
Lively discussion with mellow friends,
laughter and stories, relaxed, replete.

Happy days with paint and canvas.
Spending hours absorbed in words.
Music to soothe or lift the mood.
Meeting minds with the ancient bards.

A conscience clear, a good night's sleep,
good health, a cheerful disposition.
A love of life, no fear of death,
knowing you've made a contribution.

House Husband

The joys of redundancy 1999

They all thought that they were going fine
till the boss revealed the bottom line.
The receiver's vultures are deployed
and all the workers unemployed.

So now we have reversed the roles.
I go to work, he folds the towels.
I leave for work at seven-thirty,
come home at one all hot and dirty.

Quick bite to eat and out again,
to do the books for the IT men.
And while other folks can rest their bones
I sit up late designing homes.

If winning bread was all it takes
this role would be a piece of cake.
But there's the mortgage, phone and rates,
insurance, medicare rebates.

And just when I hope to pay the rent
the fridge becomes incontinent.
I think we're coping, doing good,
as long as we don't want any food.

Don't get me wrong, I don't complain;
he's as keen as I to work again
CVs and résumés abundant
appeared since he was made redundant.

Applications by the tonne
by fax and internet and phone.
And in the meantime, he has grasped
all the little household tasks.

Built garden walls, cleaned out the shed,
folded washing, made the bed.
Cooked the dinner, cleaned the car,
put nuts and bolts in little jars.

Shampooed the carpets, planted seeds,
put down paving, pulled up weeds.
Still I hope he'll soon be hired.
Not only work has made me tired.

This frenzied action round the home
has boosted his testosterone.

Early Saturday Morning

Early Saturday morning football,
frost on the grass and
clouds in our breath.

Thirty-six little boys chase
each other round the field
getting warm, as spectators shiver.

My daughter stamps up and down
to warm her feet,
pulls down her jumper sleeves
to cover her hands.

Dad goes to find us drinks
and we all wrap fingers gratefully
around hot cardboard cups.

I look at her, my daughter,
this younger version of me,
blond hair and perfect skin,
sipping her hot chocolate.

She is engrossed in the game,
her eyes following
her favourite player.

At the corner of her mouth
is a dusting of chocolate powder,
and my maternal instinct wants
to lick my thumb and clean away
that smudge.

But she hates it
when mothers clean their kids
with spit.

So I resist.

And I suppose
she's getting a bit old for that.
It might not be appropriate
now she's forty-one.

You Are Young

You are young.
When you should walk
you run, even in high heels.
I am old. I shuffle
when I should rush.

You are young.
You think the young boys
look cool (if that's the right word these days).
I am old. I laugh
at their ridiculous hairdos.

You are young.
You care about fashion
and how you look.
I am old, with elastic waistbands
and comfortable shoes.

You are young.
Happy to card it,
and rack up debts.
I am old. I only spend
what I actually have.

You are young.
Into all that Facebook,
Twitter and SMSs.
I am old, I still know how to write a letter
and where to buy a stamp.

You are young.
You are beautiful,
but too young to know it.
I am old, and that's okay.
It has to be.

You are young.
You rush everywhere, jaywalk through traffic,
drink your coffee on the run.

Slow down.

I am the one
who's running out of time.

Home Alone

I have the place to myself for the afternoon.
The clock is ticking,
not a sound I normally notice,
and a train has just passed on the distant line.

I am enjoying the quiet.
Hearing the background noises.
No kids, no TV, no radio.
A sort of silent movie
with no plot.

So I could decide to clean up around here,
do some laundry and ironing,
cook tea early and bake a cake.
Catch up with some bills.

But who am I kidding?
I am the world's greatest procrastinator.
If they handed out medals for it
(which they'll never get round to)
mine would be gold.

Doing nothing
is one of my favourite pastimes,
but I don't get to do it often.

I managed a little of it yesterday,
before the kids came home from school,
but I didn't get finished
so I'll do some more today.

Love and Other Catastrophes

Dining Out

We're dining out in style tonight,
my grey-haired man and me.

I watch his hazel eyes,
his features softened
by the kindly candlelight,
and smile.

He chooses something spicy
and dares his system to complain.
I order something rich and creamy
and far too high in fat.

The waiter, very young and very proper,
writes it down and then we wait.

Around us, animated conversation
in French and Dutch and Japanese.

I sip my Pinot Grigio, and he his beer.
We try to think of something bright to say
we haven't said before.

I fidget in my chair, as always, just too high.
He clears his throat and cleans his glasses
on a serviette.

Why are we ill at ease?

At least at home we sit in comfort
with the cliché
of the ageing couple,
with nothing much to say.

Falling

Inspired by a line from the song 'Fire and Blood' by the Indigo Girls
– 'I am incensed, I am in need, I am in pain, I am in love.'

I have fallen in love.
Hard.
So now I get the bit
about the heart palpitations
and staring at the moon.

I even know now
why they call it falling.

But I wasn't prepared for
the total loss
of dignity and independence,
the regression to childhood.

Stupid pet names
I'd be embarrassed
for anyone else to hear.

No one told me it spoilt
everything else in life.

I have the enthusiasm
of a sloth
and the concentration
of a goldfish.

Time with old friends,
is spent watching the clock.
Time alone always waiting
to be one half of two.

I used to enjoy
my own company.

And if all this isn't bad enough
there is the constant anxiety.

For I have heard
that there is no way back
that isn't worse than falling in.
Especially if it is the other half
who does the falling out.

Directions

You are my life's companion,
my lover and my friend
but only on my own
can I learn my way.

You are a magnet to me
and send my compass needle
spinning.

When we walk
I stagger in your footprints,
following your journey
and not my own.

I need to watch the sunset
to know which way is west.
To wait at water's edge
to read the tides.

You know these things by instinct
and you share with me
but it is not enough.
I have to feel it for myself.

You fill my senses
with abundant love
and I could drown contented
in your warmth.

But I do not fear
the quiet times alone
and I must not live in fear
of new and distant places.

So bless me
as I walk the sands
imprinted only with the waves.

Let me trust myself,
and let me stumble
for I am falling into life.

Love's Undertow

Two words from a song by Mike McClellan

Love arrives,
great waves that rise and crash
and drag us out
beyond our depth.

We learn to swim together,
drift apart,
swim together once again
through restless waves.

But on the glistening crest
a vague unrest,
that sand beneath your feet
will tempt you to the shore.

But the ocean
brings new life,
as oceans always have,
and makes us stronger.

Love is gentler now.
Ripples, where the crashing waves
once broke,
but just as deep.

The vagaries of love
can't part us now.
Only the tide
of life and death itself,

when one will dive
deeper, deeper
into universal love;

the other, wash ashore
like driftwood,
salt-crazed and gasping,
forgetting how to breathe.

Imposter

I do not like this woman
moody and sullen
and prone to tears.

Never had time
for weepy women.

She stares at me
from the glass darkly,
with her doleful expression
and bags under her eyes.

She blames her husband
her constant, loyal husband
for her misery.

Stupid woman.
He hasn't changed.

Blame the clock,
and blame the calendar.
The man is innocent.

He has the pendulum
but you have the swings.

Go away!
And let me come home
to my man.

Defying Gravity

Exercise

I am at the doctor's.
She is frowning at my cholesterol results
and my blood pressure reading.

'Do you get enough exercise?'
she asks.

Let me think.

Aerobic exercise;
jumping through hoops for the boss.

Bending and stretching;
hanging out the washing, making beds.

Resistance exercise;
trying to get the kids to eat their greens.

Flexibility and balance;
juggling work, childcare, school,
music lessons, sport, housework
and if I'm lucky, a little romance.

All working mothers do that.

I smile at her across her tidy desk.
'Probably not,' I reply.

People-watching in a City Café

The couple on the table to my left
are out to lunch for their anniversary.
No significant number. Kids are at school
and this is so much more practical
than going out in the evening.
The spark isn't really there any more.

Four skinny girls, in their smart designer clothes
and incredibly high heels, are sharing
one chocolate nut sundae and the office gossip.
Their week's wages are in the carrier bags around their feet.

The man and little boy at the table in the corner
are on an access visit, one weekend a fortnight.
But he doesn't always make it, what with work commitments.
Isn't that what caused the break-up in the first place?

He has the boy early this time;
his ex-wife is getting root canal treatment this afternoon.
He's not happy he had to take time off work
and the little guy would much rather be home with Mum
than with this stranger he calls Dad.

The couple in the opposite corner are work colleagues
pretending to themselves
that this is an innocent business lunch.
The body language says they are on the brink of an affair.
Should I go and warn them it's not worth the heartache?

The bikey boys at the long table up the back
are making a lucrative drug deal.
They cover their clandestine activity
with noisy laughter and by flirting with the waitress.

She is usually very friendly, but not today.
She is subdued and her eyes are a bit puffy.
She caught her boyfriend with her flatmate
and has moved back in with Mum and Dad.

The middle-aged lady, sitting alone, like me,
makes eye contact, smiles and quickly looks away.
Hopefully, she has given me
an interesting imaginary life.

I finish the last of my soy latte, which has gone cold,
and put away my notebook and pen.
I leave a tip for the sad waitress
and head for the station to catch the 1.45.

Growing Up

When I grow up
I can choose to be whatever I like.

I may choose to be a hammer,
working on a construction site,
building new homes or hospitals.
Folks will admire my straight nails.

But in the middle of summer
the nails would be too hot
and I might get a dreadful headache
and a circular burn on my forehead.

I may choose to be a snake.
Slithering in the undergrowth
not having to work hard at all,
gaining a certain wary respect.

But if it was a cold day, I might be very lethargic
and foolishly go and lie on the road to get warm.
One of those multi-wheel trucks might come along
and I could be left all sort of…corrugated.

I may choose to be a kite,
red, I think with a multicoloured tail.
Flying high above, seeing the world like a map.
Folks oohing and aahing at my acrobatic skill.

But I might resent the person pulling my string
and in a gust of wind, break free.
There is no saying where I would end up
or how I could possibly get home.

I don't want to be burned, or lost, or corrugated.
So if it is too hot or too cold or too windy
I might just choose to be me.

And if it is not too hot or too cold or too windy
I am quite happy being me anyway.
I may just choose…not to grow up at all.

The iCloud

The other afternoon
I think I saw the iCloud,
and as I watched, it grew,
and looked like it would burst.

Corners of photographs
poked out of its grey underside.
Treble clefs and quavers
streamed from the back
like the tail of a comet.

And on the lighter side,
still catching the sun,
I glimpsed scraps
of iridescent poetry,
metaphors and similes,
appearing and disappearing.

During the night, I was woken
by a huge bolt of lightning,
closely followed by the thunder.

Rain came down in spreadsheets,
numbers, dates and formulae
crashing and banging on the roof.

And I could feel memories,
not only my own,
running down the gutters.
soaking into the earth.

In the morning
leaves littered the garden,
windblown pages of
other people's stories,
and memories still glistened
on the grass.

The sky was clear,
not a cloud to be seen,
and my computer said,
'You are not connected
to the Internet.'

A Certain Age

I have reached a certain age
when the government treats me gently,
concessions on the pharmaceuticals
and no excuse required for sleeping in.
I are grateful, truly grateful
that I have some time for rest.

But this turning of the calendar,
this change of status,
leaves me wondering
about all the things I haven't seen
or heard or tasted.

Rivers I haven't sailed down,
mountains I could no longer climb.
Languages that will never roll
off my tongue or edify my ear.
Books I don't have time to read.

There is so much left to do.
To stand in awe before
grand monuments and works of art.
To find myself on distant shores,
or lose myself in symphonies.

To discover perhaps some talent
hidden all these years
beneath the general busyness.

It has been such a little life
and there is so much more to know.

Margaret Clark spent a nomadic childhood in the UK before migrating to South Australia. After school and college in SA, she married and moved to the Northern Territory, supposedly for three years but stayed for thirty, teaching on remote Aboriginal communities, raising two children and later retraining and working in the field of architectural drafting and design.

A move to Brisbane prompted another life change, working for the Anglican Church and studies in theology. Retirement brought her and husband, Nigel, back to SA and proximity to their family.

Margaret has been writing short stories and poetry for many years. Places, family and faith have provided much grist for the creative mill. Her poetry has been published in several anthologies by Friendly Street Poets and The Eremos Institute, and set to music for church worship.

She mentors a Writing Group in Salisbury, has been on the working party of the Salisbury Writers' Festival for several years and was co-editor for the Friendly Street Poets 2016 Anthology *Many Eyes, Many Voices*.

Frayed Edges is her first book.

www.ingramcontent.com/pod-product-compliance
Lightning Source LLC
Chambersburg PA
CBHW070913080526
44589CB00013B/1279